# A Very Simple Grammar of English

**Celia Blissett**
**Katherine Hallgarten**
with additional notes by Michael Lewis

**Language Teaching Publications**

IN TOUCH WITH TEACHERS

ISBN 0 906717 43 4

© Celia Blissett, Katherine Hallgarten
Language Teaching Publications 1985
35 Church Road. Hove BN3 2BE England

## Acknowledgements

We are grateful to Denise Chamberlain for her careful typing of a complicated manuscript.

Cover design by CDA Creative Services

Typeset in 10pt ITC Garamond.

Printed in England by Commercial Colour Press, London E7.

# Contents

**3**

# Map of this book

present simple, p16     present continuous, p17

We **live** in Grange Road but we**'re looking** for a new flat.

past simple, p18     past continuous, p19

He **rang** while I **was watching** the News.

present perfect continuous, p25     present perfect, p24

I**'ve been trying** to ring her but now I**'ve written** to her.

the future, p27

I**'m going to write** tomorrow.
I**'ll write** tomorrow.
We **leave** at six tomorrow morning.
We**'re having** lunch in Oxford.

imperative, p30     if, p92

**Ask** her **if** she needs any help.

passive, p31

The new hospital **was opened** last year.

question word questions, p55

**What** happened then?
**Who** told you?
**Where** does she live?

What **can** we do about it? *p37*

I **could** come tomorrow. *p38*

I **may** come – I'm not sure yet. *p39*

Take an umbrella – it **might** rain. *p40*

I'**ll** be there but I **won't** be staying long. *p41* *p41*

**Would** you like a cup of tea? *p42*

**Shall** I get a ticket for you? *p43*

They **should** be ready by Thursday. *p44*

I really **must** be going now. *p36*

You **ought to** see the doctor. *p45*

Do you **have to** book in advance? *(have) to, p46*

We'**ll have to** get some milk. *'ll have to, p47*

I'**ve got to** get to the bank this afternoon. *(have) got to, p48*

They'**ve got** three children now. *(have) got, p49*

I'**m not used to** such hot weather. *(be) used to, p50*

Have you **got used to** your glasses yet? *(get) used to, p50*

I **used to** live in Oxford. *used to, p51*

It's a lovely day, **isn't it.** *tags, p52*

# Map of this book

p78 p90 p78
**It's** difficult to do anything **because it's** so late.

p90
He isn't French **although** he has a French car.

p92
**If** you worked harder, you could pass!
**If** I see her I'll tell her.

p80
Is **there** a post office near here please?

p86 prepositions of time, p84
The chemist's **in** New Street is open **from** 8am **to** 10pm.

suffixes, p97 prefixes, p97
You need to **brighten** this room – why not **re-paint** it?

p100 p100
That's not his **parents'** car – that's **Jim's** own!

# The forms of the verb

In this book these terms are used:

|  | **First Form**<br>(Infinitive) | **Second Form**<br>(Past Simple) | **Third Form**<br>(Past Participle) |
|---|---|---|---|
| Regular verb | **ask** | **asked** | **asked** |
| Irregular verb | **give** | **gave** | **given** |

| | | | |
|---|---|---|---|
| FIRST<br>FORM | **ask**<br>**give** | Infinitive<br>Imperative<br>Present Simple | I'd like to **ask** him to the party.<br>**Ask!** Somebody might know.<br>Children **ask** a lot of questions. |
| SECOND<br>FORM | **asked**<br>**gave** | Past Simple | I **asked** a policeman where it was. |
| THIRD<br>FORM | **asked**<br>**given** | Present Perfect<br>Past Perfect<br>Passive | I've **asked** John to bring his car.<br>Somebody **had** already **asked** her.<br>I've **been asked** to help on Saturday. |
| THE –S<br>FORM | **asks**<br>**gives** | Present Simple<br>with *he, she, it* | Maria is at the age when she **asks** a lot of questions. |
| THE –ING<br>FORM | **asking**<br>**giving** | Verbal noun<br>Continuous forms | **Asking** too many questions annoys people.<br>Who **are** you **asking** to the party? |

We'd like everyone to **give** something.
**Give** her some flowers – she'll like that.
Most people **give** presents at Christmas.

My parents **gave** it to him.

**Have** you **given** your name to the Secretary?
They asked us but we'**d** already **given** something.
I'**ve been given** a free ticket.

He **gives** a lot of time to other people.

**Giving** is better than taking.
What **are** you **giving** her for her birthday?

# Full verbs and auxiliaries

English has two kinds of verbs: **full verbs** and **auxiliaries:**

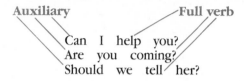

## Full verbs

- tell you 'what happened' or 'what the situation is'
- usually have four forms: **walk walks walked walking**
- an irregular verb can have five: **go goes went gone going**

Most verbs are full verbs; sometimes they are called 'ordinary verbs', or 'main' verbs. The patterns for main verbs are on pages 16 to 31.

## Auxiliaries

There are only a few auxiliaries.
**Modals: can could may might will would shall should must ought to**
The modals add extra meaning. They are on pages 36 to 45.

**Auxiliaries used to make structures**

| (be) | am | is | are | was | were | been | being |
|------|------|------|-----|---------|------|------|-------|
| (have) | has | have | had | having | | | |
| (do) | do | does | did | done | doing | | |

**(be)** always behaves like an auxiliary. Its patterns are on page 34.
**(have)** is sometimes an auxiliary and sometimes a main verb. The main verb patterns are on pages 32, 33.

| | | |
|---|---|---|
| **(be)** | present continuous, page 17 | They**'re looking** for a new flat.<br>He**'s taking** his driving test tomorrow. |
| | past continuous, page 19 | **Was** he **watching** us?<br>Who **were** they **waiting** for? |
| | passive, page 31 | They **are made** of pure silk.<br>It **was built** in 1937. |
| | + *going to,* page 27 | I think it**'s going to** rain.<br>**Were** you **going to** tell him? |
| **(have)** | present perfect, page 24 | He**'s lost** his glasses.<br>I**'ve** never **eaten** passion fruit before.<br>We **hadn't taken** a map, so we got lost. |
| | past perfect, page 25 | |
| | (have) got, page 49 | **Have** you **got** tickets?<br>I **hadn't got** my passport with me. |
| **(do)** | negative of a full verb<br>    – present<br>    – past | I **don't understand.**<br>We **didn't bring** the car after all. |
| | questions with a full verb – present<br>                    – past | **Do** you **eat** meat?<br>**Did** they **come** by plane? |
| | emphasis with a full verb – present<br>                  – past | I **do like** your hair.<br>We **did enjoy** ourselves. |
| | instead of repeating a full verb | I like my coffee strong.<br>▷ So **do** I.<br>Jayne went but Joyce **didn't.** |

# Auxiliaries

These words, called the modal auxiliaries, are used *only* as auxiliaries:

| | |
|---|---|
| **can** | I **can't** tell you – it's a secret. |
| **could** | Nobody **could** tell me your phone number. |
| **may** | It **may** rain later. |
| **might** | We **might** go to Spain for our holidays this year. |
| **will** | When **will** we get to London? |
| **would** | What **would** you like for your birthday? |
| **shall** | **Shall** I put the light on? |
| **should** | I think we **should** buy her a small present. |
| **must** | I **must** be going soon. |

Important structures using auxiliaries:

### 1. Making negatives:

Add **n't** at the end of the first auxiliary; if there is no auxiliary use **(do)**.

| | |
|---|---|
| He could drive. | He **couldn't** drive. |
| He drives. He does drive. | He **doesn't** drive. |

### 2. Making questions:

Change the order of the subject and the first auxiliary; if there is no auxiliary use **(do)**.

| | |
|---|---|
| We should try to ring her. | **Should** we **try** to ring her? |
| He drives. He does drive. | **Does** he **drive?** |

### 3. Making a tag:

Use the first auxiliary; if there is no auxiliary use **(do)**.

| | |
|---|---|
| It's a lovely day. | It's a lovely day, **isn't** it. |
| He drives. | He drives, **doesn't** he? |

## 4. Making a short answer:

Use the first auxiliary; if there is no auxiliary use (**do**).

| | | |
|---|---|---|
| Have you heard from Paul? | ▷ Yes I **have.** | ▷ No I **haven't.** |
| Will Jill be there? | ▷ Yes she **will.** | ▷ No she **won't.** |
| Do you know where it is? | ▷ Yes I **do.** | ▷ No I **don't.** |

## 5. Making an interested response:

Use the first auxiliary in the answer; if there is no auxiliary use (**do**).

| | |
|---|---|
| I've been there before. | ▷ Oh, **have** you? |
| He was looking for you. | ▷ Oh, **was** he? |
| She drives an old Fiat. | ▷ Oh, **does** she? |
| We caught the early train. | ▷ Oh, **did** you? |

## 6. Emphasis, to show special emotion:

Stress the first auxiliary; if there is no auxiliary use (**do**).

I've been waiting 10 minutes.
→ I **have** been waiting 10 minutes.

I know the way.
→ I **do** know the way.

I can come tomorrow.
→ I **can** come tomorrow.

I waited more than an hour.
→ I **did** wait more than an hour.

## A general rule of spoken English:

Certain patterns are **always** used exactly the same way. If a pattern uses an auxiliary, and a sentence does not have an auxiliary: use part of (**do**) – *do, does, did* – and follow the same pattern. Some books call (**do**) the "dummy auxiliary."

# Short and full forms

## Short forms

Normal speech (*I'm sorry*)
Informal writing (letters to friends)

## Full forms

Stress in speech (*I **am** sorry*)
At the end of a sentence. (*Yes, I am.*)
In questions. (*Are you going?*)
Most writing.

### The verb (be)

| | | | | | |
|---|---|---|---|---|---|
| I'm | you're | he's | I am | you are | he is |
| I'm not | you're not/<br>you aren't | he isn't | I am not | you are not | he is not |

### The verb (have)

| | | | | | |
|---|---|---|---|---|---|
| we've | she's | they'd | we have | she has | they had |
| we haven't | he hadn't | she hasn't | we have not | he had not | she has not |

### The verb (do)

| | |
|---|---|
| she doesn't | she does not |
| they don't | they do not |
| we didn't | we did not |

### Will

| | |
|---|---|
| I'll | I will |
| I won't | I will not |

### Would

| | |
|---|---|
| they'd | they would |
| they wouldn't | they would not |

The short forms:

**'s**  can be **is**  It*'s* raining.  She*'s* waiting.
        or **has**  He*'s* remembered.  Jack*'s* taken it.

**'d**  can be **had**  He*'d* already gone.  Who*'d* you told?
        or **would**  I*'d* like to go.  They*'d* never believe you.

In normal speech the short, unstressed, forms are used.

The stressed form adds *extra* meaning.

| | |
|---|---|
| I'm sorry. | Normal |
| I **am** sorry. | Stronger, more serious apology |
| | |
| I've been waiting an hour. | Fact |
| I **have** been waiting an hour. | Slightly annoyed |
| | |
| She's left. | Fact |
| She **has** left. | Correcting what the other person says or thinks |
| | |
| That was nice. | Fact, a bit cool |
| That **was** nice. | Enthusiastic |

# Present simple

| I you we they | walk<br>don't walk |
|---|---|
| he she it | **walks**<br>doesn't walk |

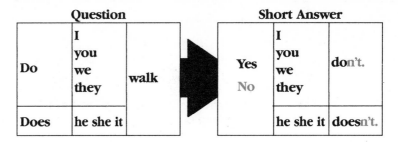

| | Question | | | | Short Answer | | |
|---|---|---|---|---|---|---|---|
| Do | I you we they | walk | | Yes<br>No | I you we they | don't. |
| Does | he she it | | | | he she it | doesn't. |

I usually **get up** about seven.

Does Tony **drive** to work?
▷ No, he **cycles.**

The football season usually **starts** in August.

Regular actions or events

I **like** tea but I **don't like** milk in it!

What **does** this **mean** please?

The River Danube **flows** through Vienna.

Facts

Next Monday **is** a national holiday.

Classes **begin** next week.

Facts known about the future

I **don't want** to go out this evening.

I'm sorry I **don't understand.**

I **feel** sick.

Thoughts and feelings at the time of speaking

| | | | | | **Question** | | | | | **Short Answer** | |
|---|---|---|---|---|---|---|---|---|---|---|---|
| I | 'm not | | | Am | I | | | | I | am.<br>'m not. | |
| he she it | isn't<br>'s not | coming | | Is | he she it | coming | | Yes<br>No | he she it | isn't. | |
| we<br>you<br>they | 're not<br>aren't | | | Are | we<br>you<br>they | | | | we<br>you<br>they | aren't. | |

**'re not** is used more than **aren't.**

Look, Mary**'s getting** into that car.          At the time of speaking
I**'m not looking forward to** the interview.
Excuse me, **is** anyone **sitting** here, please?
Who**'s** Katy **talking** to?

They**'re building** a block of flats over there.   True at the moment, but not always
We**'re looking for** a new house.
**Is** your baby **sleeping** all night yet?
▷ No she **isn't,** not yet.

Karim**'s working** on night shift next week.    Present plans for the future
When **are** they **flying** to India?
**Are** you **coming** to the party on Saturday?
▷ No, I**'m not** as a matter of fact.

# Past simple

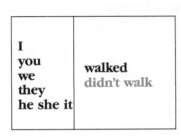

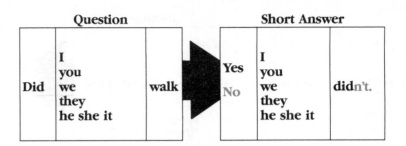

For important verbs with different forms in the past simple – see p20 to 23.

| | |
|---|---|
| Stefan **wanted** to catch the early train but he **missed** it. | Single actions, thoughts or feelings finished before the time of speaking |
| I **told** you it **started** at 7 o'clock. I **knew** it did. | |
| Where **did** you **go** last night?<br>▷ We **went** to the pub for a drink. | |
| **Did** you **lock** the door?<br>▷ Yes, I **did,** don't worry. | |
| They **told** me I **needed** to wear glasses. | Reporting what someone said (after verbs like *said, told, asked*) |
| Why **didn't** you **tell** him?<br>▷ He **said** he **knew** about it already. | |

| | | |
|---|---|---|
| I<br>he she it | wasn't | |
| | | waiting |
| you<br>we<br>they | weren't | |

**Question**

| | | |
|---|---|---|
| Was | I<br>he she it | |
| | | waiting |
| Were | we<br>you<br>they | |

**Short Answer**

Yes / No

| | |
|---|---|
| I<br>he she it | wasn't. |
| you<br>we<br>they | weren't. |

I **was watching** the News when you rang.

What **were** you **doing** when you heard the crash?
▷ I **was getting** dressed.

An event, finished before the moment of speaking, which went on for a period.

I **was** just **thinking** of ringing him when he walked in.

We got married while we **were living** in York.

**Were** they **waiting** when you got there?
▷ No, they **weren't.**

Often the *longer* of two actions is in the past continuous and the *shorter* in the past simple.

**19**

# Irregular verbs

There are about 180 irregular verbs. Some are very unusual. Here are the most useful.

| First form | Second form | Third form | First form | Second form | Third form |
|---|---|---|---|---|---|
| be | was, were | been | find | found | found |
| beat | beat | beaten | fly | flew | flown |
| become | became | become | forget | forgot | forgotten |
| begin | began | begun | forgive | forgave | forgiven |
| bend | bent | bent | freeze | froze | frozen |
| bite | bit | bitten | | | |
| blow | blew | blown | get | got | got |
| break | broke | broken | give | gave | given |
| bring | brought | brought | go | went | gone |
| build | built | built | grow | grew | grown |
| buy | bought | bought | | | |
| | | | have | had | had |
| catch | caught | caught | hear | heard | heard |
| choose | chose | chosen | hide | hid | hidden |
| come | came | come | hit | hit | hit |
| cost | cost | cost | hold | held | held |
| cut | cut | cut | hurt | hurt | hurt |
| | | | keep | kept | kept |
| do | did | done | know | knew | known |
| draw | drew | drawn | | | |
| drink | drank | drunk | lend | lent | lent |
| drive | drove | driven | leave | left | left |
| | | | let | let | let |
| eat | ate | eaten | light | lit | lit |
| | | | lose | lost | lost |
| fall | fell | fallen | | | |
| feed | fed | fed | make | made | made |
| feel | felt | felt | mean | meant | meant |
| fight | fought | fought | meet | met | met |

| First form | Second form | Third form | First form | Second form | Third form |
|---|---|---|---|---|---|
| pay | paid | paid | steal | stole | stolen |
| put | put | put | stick | stuck | stuck |
| | | | | | |
| ride | rode | ridden | take | took | taken |
| read | read | read | teach | taught | taught |
| ring | rang | rung | tear | tore | torn |
| run | ran | run | tell | told | told |
| | | | think | thought | thought |
| say | said | said | throw | threw | thrown |
| see | saw | seen | | | |
| sell | sold | sold | understand | understood | understood |
| send | sent | sent | | | |
| set | set | set | wake | woke | woken |
| shake | shook | shaken | wear | wore | worn |
| shine | shone | shone | win | won | won |
| shoot | shot | shot | write | wrote | written |
| show | showed | shown | | | |
| shrink | shrank | shrunk | | | |
| shut | shut | shut | | | |
| sing | sang | sung | | | |
| sit | sat | sat | | | |
| sleep | slept | slept | | | |
| speak | spoke | spoken | | | |
| spend | spent | spent | | | |
| split | split | split | | | |
| spoil | spoilt | spoilt | | | |
| stand | stood | stood | | | |

Some verbs have two spellings:

**burnt** or **burned**
**smelt** or **smelled**

The verbs are:

| | | |
|---|---|---|
| burn | smell | learn |
| dream | spell | spill |

# Irregular verbs

Here the same verbs are in groups to make them easy to learn.

| First form | Second form | Third form | First form | Second form | Third form |
|---|---|---|---|---|---|
| **All forms the same** | | | blow | blew | blown |
| cost | cost | cost | fly | flew | flown |
| cut | cut | cut | know | knew | known |
| hit | hit | hit | throw | threw | thrown |
| hurt | hurt | hurt | grow | grew | grown |
| let | let | let | draw | drew | drawn |
| put | put | put | | | |
| set | set | set | | | |
| shut | shut | shut | begin | began | begun |
| split | split | split | drink | drank | drunk |
| | | | ring | rang | rung |
| **Similar sound groups** | | | sing | sang | sung |
| beat | beat | beaten | shrink | shrank | shrunk |
| bite | bit | bitten | | | |
| eat | ate | eaten | freeze | froze | frozen |
| fall | fell | fallen | speak | spoke | spoken |
| forget | forgot | forgotten | steal | stole | stolen |
| forgive | forgave | forgiven | break | broke | broken |
| give | gave | given | wake | woke | woken |
| hide | hid | hidden | choose | chose | chosen |
| shake | shook | shaken | drive | drove | driven |
| take | took | taken | write | wrote | written |
| tear | tore | torn | ride | rode | ridden |
| wear | wore | worn | | | |

| First form | Second form | Third form |
|---|---|---|
| **Second and third forms the same** | | |
| bend | bent | bent |
| build | built | built |
| feel | felt | felt |
| keep | kept | kept |
| leave | left | left |
| light | lit | lit |
| lend | lent | lent |
| mean | meant | meant |
| meet | met | met |
| send | sent | sent |
| shoot | shot | shot |
| sleep | slept | slept |
| spend | spent | spent |
| spoil | spoilt | spoilt |
| get | got | got |
| lose | lost | lost |
| sit | sat | sat |
| | | |
| bring | brought | brought |
| buy | bought | bought |
| fight | fought | fought |
| think | thought | thought |
| catch | caught | caught |
| teach | taught | taught |

| First form | Second form | Third form |
|---|---|---|
| feed | fed | fed |
| find | found | found |
| have | had | had |
| hear | heard | heard |
| hold | held | held |
| make | made | made |
| pay | paid | paid |
| read | read | read |
| say | said | said |
| sell | sold | sold |
| stand | stood | stood |
| understand | understood | understood |
| tell | told | told |
| stick | stuck | stuck |
| win | won | won |
| shine | shone | shone |
| **All forms different** | | |
| be | was/were | been |
| become | became | become |
| come | came | come |
| do | did | done |
| go | went | gone |
| run | ran | run |
| see | saw | seen |
| show | showed | shown |

**23**

# Present perfect

What have you done to your hair!

| I you we they | (have) 've haven't | gone |
|---|---|---|
| he she it | (has) 's hasn't | |

**Question**

| Have | I you we they | gone |
|---|---|---|
| Has | he she it | |

**Short Answer**

| Yes No | I you we they | haven't. |
|---|---|---|
| | he she it | hasn't. |

**We haven't seen** Tom for a long time.

**Has** Paula **taken** her driving test yet?
▷ No, she **hasn't.**

**Have** you ever **been** to the Tower of London?
▷ Yes, but I **haven't been** there for twenty years!

I've never **heard** that before.

The speaker is looking back from the present to the past.

24

# Present perfect continuous

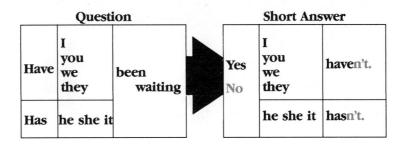

**Have** you **been waiting** long?

How long **have** you **been learning** English?

I**'ve been thinking** of changing my job.

Carmen **hasn't been feeling** too well recently.

Why are you crying?
▷ I**'ve been chopping** onions.

You don't look surprised.
▷ I'm not. I**'ve been expecting** this to happen.

The speaker is looking back from the present to a period in the past. The period is continuing at the moment of speaking or has stopped.

# Past perfect

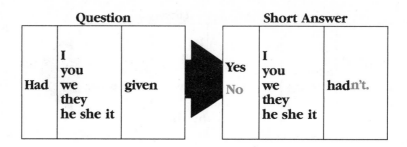

| I you we they he she it | 'd hadn't | given |
|---|---|---|

**Question**

| Had | I you we they he she it | given |
|---|---|---|

**Short Answer**

| Yes No | I you we they he she it | hadn't. |
|---|---|---|

**I hadn't met** him until the meeting last week.

He got the job because he**'d learned** to type.

I**'d** never **seen** snow until I came to England.

We**'d finished** by twelve o'clock.

The speaker is looking back from the past on the earlier past.

There is no special verb form to talk about the future in English.

| We | 're going to leave<br>'ll leave<br>'re leaving<br>leave | at seven o'clock tomorrow morning. |

All these are correct. They give the same facts. The choice depends on the *reason* the speaker sees for the future event.

## (be) going to

**I'm going to give up smoking.**

| I | 'm not | |
|---|---|---|
| you<br>we<br>they | 're not<br>aren't | going to<br>come |
| he she it | 's not<br>isn't | |

**Question**

| Am | I | |
|---|---|---|
| Are | you<br>we<br>they | going to<br>come |
| Is | he she it | |

Yes

No

**Short Answer**

| | I | am.<br>'m not. |
|---|---|---|
| | you<br>we<br>they | aren't. |
| | he she it | isn't. |

Oh dear, **I'm going to sneeze.**

Look at those clouds – it**'s going to rain.**

There is evidence ( *a tickle, clouds*) now for the future event.

She**'s going to change** her job.

What **are** you **going to do** this evening?
▷ **I'm going to watch** the film on TV.

There is a long-term *decision* about the future.

# The Future

'll

**I won't be a moment, I'll just get my jacket.**

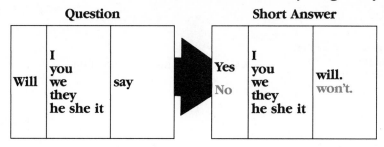

| I you we they he she it | 'll won't | say |
|---|---|---|

**Question**

| Will | I you we they he she it | say |
|---|---|---|

**Short Answer**

| Yes No | I you we they he she it | will. won't. |
|---|---|---|

On the fast train they**'ll arrive** at 8 o'clock.

It looks as if it**'ll be** a nice weekend.

There **won't be** a Christmas party this year.

Something the speaker thinks is certain to happen.

I'm tired. I think I**'ll go** to bed.

**Will** Maria **be** back soon?
▷ No, she **won't be** back today, but she**'ll be** here all day tomorrow.

What **will** you do?

When **will** you **get** your results?
▷ I **won't know** before the end of August.

The speaker's opinion, or decision or feeling formed at the moment of speaking.

## Present continuous

What time **are** you **leaving** tomorrow?
▷ We**'re getting** the 6.50 train.
I**'m working** late every evening next week.
They**'re going** out this evening.

## Present simple

My birthday **is** on a Wednesday this year.
Christmas Day **falls** on a Sunday this year.
Ramadan **ends** in two weeks time.

## I'm playing tennis on Saturday.

The speaker *knows* because of something which has already happened, usually an arrangement with another person.

## The Cup Final is on May 17th this year.

Events fixed by the calendar or an official timetable. A fact you can look up.

# Imperative

**Come in! Don't wait outside.**

There is no special form of the verb for the imperative in English.

**Mix** the flour and the sugar.                  Instructions

**Take** two tablets every four hours.

**Take** the second turning on the left.

**Come** in, **make** yourselves at home.         Invitations

Please **start, don't wait** for me.

**Open** your books, **turn** to page 5 and        Telling someone what to do
**look at** the first picture.                      (instructions or orders)

**Hurry up!** It's twenty past seven.

**Don't forget** to post that letter!

**Don't be** late!

**Push.**                                          Signs and notices

**Insert** 2 × 50p.

**Keep off** the grass.

**Note**
To suggest doing something together use *Let's*.  **Let's** go now or we'll be late.
                                                    **Let's** take the car.

Two negatives are possible:                        **Let's not** tell Jenny, she'll only worry.
                                                    **Don't let's** tell Jenny, she'll only worry.

**30**

## Present

| I | 'm not | |
| he she it | 's isn't | asked |
| we you they | 're aren't | |

### Question

| Am | I | |
| Is | he she it | asked |
| Are | we you they | |

## Past

| I he she it | wasn't | |
| we you they | weren't | asked |

### Question

| Was | I he she it | |
| Were | we you they | asked |

## Perfect

| I you we they | haven't | been asked |
| he she it | hasn't | |

### Question

| Have | I you we they | been asked |
| Has | he she it | |

The **Short Answers** are made in the usual way:
**Were** they **made** in India?  ▷ **Yes, they were.**
**Have** you **been offered** the job?  ▷ **No, I haven't**

The passive is usual if *who* did the action is not known, or is not as important as *what* happened. It is also used if "a general group" of people did the action.

These shoes **were made** in Brazil.
Football **is played** all over the world.
**Have** you **been invited** to the wedding?
**Has** Jill **been told** yet?

It **was opened** by the Queen last year.
The packet **was sent** more than a week ago.
**Has** it **been damaged?**

# The verb (have)

## Present

| I you we they | 've haven't |
|---|---|
| he she it | 's hasn't |

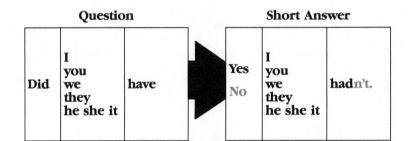

**Question**

| Do | I you we they | have |
|---|---|---|
| Does | he she it | |

Yes
No

**Short Answer**

| I you we they | haven't. |
|---|---|
| he she it | hasn't. |

## Past

| I you we they he she it | hadn't |
|---|---|

**Question**

| Did | I you we they he she it | have |
|---|---|---|

Yes
No

**Short Answer**

| I you we they he she it | hadn't. |
|---|---|

# (have) – full verb

When **(have)** is used as a full verb it makes questions and negatives like all other full verbs.

**Did** you **have** a good weekend?          Pass time, experience
**Have** a good trip!
**Are** you **having** trouble with that?

What **do** you usually **have** for breakfast?          Meals, food, drink
**Do** you **have** lunch at work?
What shall we **have** for dinner?
**Have** you **had** something to drink?

I'm going to **have** a shower.          With *bath, shower*

# (have) – auxiliary

When **(have)** is used as an auxiliary, use the patterns on pages 12 and 13.

**Have** you **brought** your bike with you?          To make perfect verb forms, see p24, 25, 26.
What a surprise! I **hadn't expected** that!

**Note**
**(have)** is not normally used for possession, **have got** is usually used.

**(have) to**          see page 46
**(have) got to**          see page 48
**(have) got**          see page 49

# The verb (be)

am, is, are, was, were, been, being

## Present

| I | 'm not |
|---|---|
| you<br>we<br>they | 're not<br>aren't |
| he she it | 's<br>isn't |

### Question

| Am | I |
|---|---|
| Are | you<br>we<br>they |
| Is | he she it |

### Short Answer

| Yes | I | am.<br>'m not. |
|---|---|---|
| No | you<br>we<br>they | aren't. |
| | he she it | isn't. |

## Past

| I<br>he she it | wasn't |
|---|---|
| you<br>we<br>they | weren't |

### Question

| Was | I<br>he she it |
|---|---|
| Were | you<br>we<br>they |

### Short Answer

| Yes | I<br>he she it | wasn't. |
|---|---|---|
| No | you<br>we<br>they | weren't. |

John **is** four now.
Omar **was** a builder in Iran.

(be) as a full verb

**Are** you **coming** with us?
He **was doing** 75 when the police stopped him.
**Have** you **been waiting** long?

(be) as an auxiliary to make continuous verb forms (see p17, 19, 25, 108/9)

The bridge **was opened** by the Queen last year.
My car **has been stolen.**

(be) as an auxiliary to make passive verb forms (see p31)

**do, does, did, done, doing**

# The verb (do)

## Present

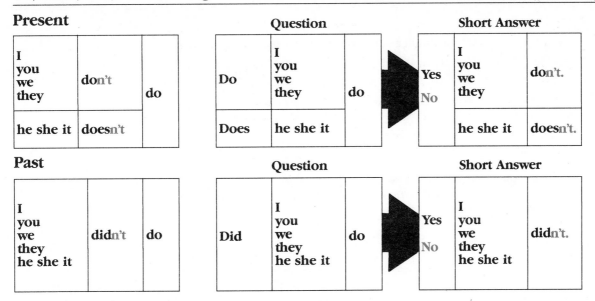

| I you we they | don't | do |
|---|---|---|
| he she it | doesn't | |

**Question**

| Do | I you we they | do |
|---|---|---|
| Does | he she it | |

**Short Answer**

| Yes | I you we they | don't. |
|---|---|---|
| No | he she it | doesn't. |

## Past

| I you we they he she it | didn't | do |
|---|---|---|

**Question**

| Did | I you we they he she it | do |
|---|---|---|

**Short Answer**

| Yes | I you we they he she it | didn't. |
|---|---|---|
| No | | |

(**do**) is used both as an auxiliary and as a full verb.
The full verb uses are marked in these examples.

Do you **do** your own cooking?
Who is going to **do** the washing?
Paul **did** his homework but Ann didn't **do** hers.
Did you **do** anything exciting at the weekend?

Did you **do** those letters?
▷ I'm afraid I haven't **done** them yet.

What do you **do?**
▷ I'm a nurse.

The most common use of (**do**) is as the 'dummy auxiliary' in English. It is used like the other auxiliaries to make questions, negatives, tags and other structures. See p12/13.

**35**

# Modal auxiliaries

**1.** Modals are never about facts.

**2.** They are about the speaker's or listener's opinion *at the moment of speaking.*

> *David has long hair* is about David. It is a fact.
> *David must get his hair cut* is about David. It is also about the *speaker's opinion.*

> Questions with a modal are about the *listener's opinion:*
> *What should I do?* (= What do *you* think is the best thing to do?)

**3.** They can refer to past time or future time.

| | |
|---|---|
| I **could ride** a bike when I was five. | Past time |
| I **could come** tomorrow. | Future time |
| You **must speak** French. (I know you took lessons). | Past time |
| If you're going to live in France you **must speak** French. (You'll have to learn). | Future time |

# must

| | |
|---|---|
| **I must** remember to post this letter. | The speaker's view of what is necessary |
| You **must** read this book – it's really good. | |
| She **mustn't** go out until she's better. | |
| | |
| When **must** we be there? | Asking for the listener's view of what is necessary |
| **Must** you **make** so much noise? | |
| | |
| I don't know her age but she **must** be over 60. | Deduction, logically necessary |
| You **must** be tired after such a long journey. | |
| This **must** be the right road. | |

**Can** always refers to different kinds of possibility.

| | |
|---|---|
| **Can** you **come** round on Friday evening? <br> ▷ I'm afraid I **can't** manage Friday. <br><br> **Can** you **tell** me the way to the Post Office, please? <br> ▷ I'm sorry I **can't**. I'm a stranger here. <br><br> **Can** you **drive?** <br> ▷ Yes, I **can.** | Possibility |
| You **can't** park on a double yellow line. <br><br> **Can** I leave work early today please? <br><br> **Can** we bring the children with us? | Possibility decided by law or rules |
| **Can** you pass the salt please? <br><br> **Can** you give me a hand with this please? | Requests (*Is it possible for you to . . . ?*) |
| **Can** I get a ticket for you? <br><br> **Can** we give you a lift? | Offers (*Is it possible for me to . . . for you?*) |
| You **can't** be hungry. You've just had a big lunch. <br><br> Anna **can't** have gone home. Her bag's still here. | Deduction – logical possibility. Always with *can't* (negative) |

# could

*Could*, like *can*, is about possibility. *Could* is more *remote* than *can*; remote relationships (polite requests), remote in time, or more remote logical possibility.

**Could** I speak to Hilary, please?

**Could** I have six of those oranges, please?

Polite requests

Gerda **could** read when she was four.

Possibility in the past

**Could** you get a seat on the train?
▷ I'm afraid we **couldn't.** It was very crowded.

We **couldn't** find anywhere to park.

You **couldn't** change money without your passport.

Is that Carol over there?
▷ I'm not sure – it **could** be.

Do you think Paul **could** have gone home already?

You **could** have left it on the bus.

I'm sure you **couldn't** have left it on the bus.

Take a sweater. It **could** turn cold later.

In these examples *could* is similar in meaning to *might*. Logical possibility; something *might* be true.

You **may** have dropped it in the supermarket.    Likely, but not certain. (1)

I'd take a coat – it **may** turn cold later.

I **may** not have time to phone you this evening.

Do you think it was John we saw earlier?
▷ It **may** have been, I'm not sure.

**May** I borrow your dictionary for a moment, please?    Asking for permission. (2)

**May** we have a few days to think about it?

**Note**
*Mayn't* is very unusual: *may not* is usually used.

# might

I don't feel very well.
▷ It **might** be something you've eaten.

Where are you going for your holidays?
▷ I'm not sure; we **might** go to Scotland.

I'm surprised Chris isn't here yet. Do you think he **might** have forgotten?

I'm leaving early tomorrow so I **might** not see you.

Is this a 24 bus coming?
▷ It **might** be. I can't see the number yet.

Likely, but not certain.
Similar to *may* in (1) on p39.

**Note**
*Mightn't* is unusual.

## will + n't = won't

| | |
|---|---|
| **Will** you sign the form, please?<br>**Will** you phone me when you arrive? | Asking someone to do something *(Will you . . .?)* |
| I **will** if I have time. | Agreeing |
| I**'ll** give you a hand with that.<br>We**'ll** do the washing-up. | Offering to do something for someone |
| She **won't** tell me where she's going tonight.<br>I **won't** work on that machine. It's dangerous.<br>Molly's car **won't** start.<br>The baby **won't** stop crying. | Refusing |
| We **won't** see you next week. We**'ll** be on holiday.<br>I**'ll** be back in a few minutes. | Facts about the future |
| Wait a minute! I**'ll** just get a sweater.<br>That's the doorbell – It**'ll** be John.<br>I**'ll** have pizza and salad, please. | Immediate decisions at the moment of speaking |
| You**'ll** catch the train if you leave now.<br>You **won't** be happy if you don't buy it! | Likely conditions, see page 92 |

**Note**
*Will not* is very strong. In speech the normal form is *won't*.

# would

Would you drop me at the station please?                    Requests

Would you mind closing the window please?

Would you mind if I came a few minutes late?

Would you like a cup of tea?                                Offers and invitations

Would you like to come with us?
▷ That's very kind of you. I'd love to.

Would you like some more cake?
▷ No thank you, I'm fine but it's very nice.

What would be the best thing to do?                         Advice

What would you do?
▷ If I were you I'd see the doctor.

They wouldn't stop the noise even when I asked.            Refusing

My car wouldn't start this morning.

I don't know what was wrong with the baby, but
she wouldn't stop crying.

You wouldn't enjoy the film, I don't think.               Talking about a hypothetical situation

Shall I bring my sleeping bag?
▷ That would help.

| | |
|---|---|
| **Shall** we pick you up at the station? | Offering to do something |
| **Shall** I get a ticket for you? | |
| **Shall** we go for a walk after lunch? | Suggestions |
| Who **shall** we ask to the party? | |
| What **shall** we do about it? | |

**Note**

*Shall* is unusual in modern English except in questions with *Shall I . . . ?* and *Shall we . . . ?*

# should

You **should** tell the police about it.

I think you **should** go to the doctor.
▷ Perhaps I **should.**

If you don't feel better you **should** go to bed.

The train **should** be there by four o'clock.

Excuse me, I think it **should** be £2, not £3.

You **should** have told me that you don't eat meat.

Kurt **shouldn't** have left without paying.

The *speaker's* view of the correct situation, or thing to do.

Do you think I **should** tell Peter?

What do you think I **should** do?

*Asking* the *listener's* view of the correct thing to do.

**Note**
Questions with *Should I/we . . .?* are unusual; *Do you think I/we should . . . ?* is the usual form.

# ought to

| I<br>you<br>we<br>they<br>he she it | ought not to | take |
|---|---|---|

Question forms are very unusual (see below).

I **ought to** ring my mother.

You **ought to** phone your parents.

What do you think we **ought to** do about it?

People **ought not to** park here – it's dangerous.

Obligation (usually moral)

**Note**

*Oughtn't* is unusual; the usual form is *ought not.*

Questions like *Ought we to . . . . ?* are very unusual; the usual form is *Do you think we ought to . . . ?*

# (have) to

## Present

| I you we they | don't have to | ask |
|---|---|---|
| he she it | has to / doesn't have to | |

### Question

| Do | I you we they | have to | ask |
|---|---|---|---|
| Does | he she it | | |

### Short Answer

| Yes No | I you we they | don't. |
|---|---|---|
| | he she it | doesn't. |

## Past

| I you we they he she it | had to / didn't have to | ask |
|---|---|---|

### Question

| Did | I you we they he she it | have to | ask |
|---|---|---|---|

### Short Answer

| Yes No | I you we they he she it | didn't. |
|---|---|---|

Children over 14 **have to** pay full price.
The doctor says he **has to** stay in bed.
Did you **have to** wait long?
You **have to** be at the airport very early
because they **have to** search all the bags.

**Necessity based on:**
a rule
an authority
circumstances

**Note**
*(have) to* is used for *objective* necessity; *must* for what the *speaker thinks* is necessary.

We *have to* be there by four o'clock.
We *must* be there by four o'clock.

Suggests: *They close the doors at four.*
Suggests: *I think all the seats will be taken by four.*

## I'll have to get some more coffee.

We**'ll have to** paint the house before we sell it.

We**'ll have to** go or we'll miss the last bus.

It's broken – you**'ll have to** buy a new one.

I'm afraid she**'ll have to** go into hospital.

The speaker's idea of something necessary

## Negatives

**don't have to** = it is *not necessary* that . . .

You **don't have to** buy a ticket.
We **didn't have to** wait at all.

**mustn't** = it is *necessary not* to . . .

I **mustn't** forget to post this letter.
You **mustn't** take more than two of these pills at a time.

**Note**

*Don't have to* and *Don't need to* are very similar in meaning:

I'm sure we *don't need to* ask. = I'm sure we *don't have to* ask.

You *don't have to* be here before 9. = You *don't need to* be here before 9.

# (have) got to

## Present

| I you we they | 've haven't | got to take |
|---|---|---|
| he she it | 's hasn't | |

**Question**

| Have | I you we they | got to take |
|---|---|---|
| Has | he she it | |

**Short Answer**

| Yes No | I you we they | haven't. |
|---|---|---|
| | he she it | hasn't. |

He**'s got to** stay in bed for a few days.

You**'ve got to** put two 10 pence coins in to make it work.

I **haven't got to** get up early in the morning.

Sorry I can't stop – I**'ve got to** get to the bank before half past three.

**Have** we **got to** show our passports?


**Note**
*(have) to* and *(have) got to* are used with the same meaning.
*had got to* is unusual in the past; *had to* is normally used.

*(have)* is not normally used to talk about possession; *(have) got* is normally used.
*(have) got* makes questions and negatives using *(have)* as auxiliary.
*had got* is unusual in the past; *had* is normally used.

### Present

| I you we they | 've haven't | got |
|---|---|---|
| he she it | 's hasn't | |

### Question

| Have | I we you they | got |
|---|---|---|
| Has | he she it | |

### Short Answer

| Yes No | I you we they | haven't. |
|---|---|---|
| | he she it | hasn't. |

### Past

| I you we they he she it | 'd hadn't | got |
|---|---|---|

### Question

| Had | I you we they he she it | got |
|---|---|---|

### Short Answer

| Yes No | I you we they he she it | hadn't. |
|---|---|---|

We **haven't got** a phone.
Anna**'s got** dark hair and blue eyes.
**Have** you **got** change for a pound please?
▷ I'm afraid I **haven't**.
They **hadn't got** any apples so I bought
some pears instead.

                                     Possession

**Have** you **got** a free evening next week?
Excuse me, **have** you **got** a minute please?
**Have** you **got** an appointment?

                                     Certain expressions of time

# (be) used to, (get) used to

I'**m used to** gett**ing** up early. | To talk about what is normal

He'**s not used to** driv**ing** on the left.

We **aren't used to** very hot weather in England.

How's your new job? | To talk about the process of changing
▷ Oh I'**m getting used to** it, thank you. | to a new normal situation

**Have** you **got used to** our winters yet?
▷ I'**m getting used to** them, slowly!

I **was** just **getting used to** my old job
when they moved me.

I don't like this new medicine.
▷ Don't worry. I'm sure you'**ll** soon **get used to** it.

**Note**
*(be) used to* and *(get) used to* use these patterns:

| He | **isn't** **hasn't got** | **used to** | his new job yet. | (noun) |
| | | | it. | (pronoun) |
| | | | living in London. | (. . . *ing* form) |

**used to** + first form, *I used to live in London,* has a different meaning; see page 51.

| I<br>you<br>we<br>they<br>he she it | used to<br>didn't use to | live |
|---|---|---|

Question forms are unusual.

I **used to** smoke.

He **used to** play squash until his accident.

Do you work full time?
▷ Not now, but I **used to** before I had the children.

It's funny. I really enjoy cricket now but I **didn't use to.**

Something which was true for a period in the past but was not true later

Note
*Did you use to . . . ?* is unusual; we usually say *You used to . . . , didn't you?*

# Tags

Tags are very important in spoken English. They are not used in written English.

| Say | Mean |
|-----|------|
| It's a lovely day, **isn't it.** | Say something about the weather. |
| That was a super film, **wasn't it.** | Say something about the film. |
| That's a good idea, **isn't it.** | Give me your opinion about it. |
| Things were different then, **weren't they.** | Talk about your memory of the situation. |

Tags are not questions. They usually invite the other person to make a comment.

## How to make tags

Use the first auxiliary to make the tag. If there is no auxiliary use *do, does* or *did*.

| Positive sentence | Negative tag | Negative sentence | Positive tag |
|-------------------|--------------|-------------------|--------------|
| It's a beautiful day, | **isn't it.** | It **isn't** a very nice morning, | **is it.** |
| You've been to London, | **haven't you.** | You **haven't** been to London, | **have you.** |
| It **must** have been David, | **mustn't it.** | It **couldn't** have been David, | **could it.** |
| You **know** Mary, | **don't you.** | They **don't** eat pork, | **do they.** |
| She **drives** to work, | **doesn't she.** | Your mother **doesn't** speak English, | **does she.** |
| They **played** well, | **didn't they.** | You **didn't** leave the window open, | **did you.** |

Most tags ask the other person to *comment*. If you say them like questions they ask the other person to *confirm* what you think:

| **Say** | **Mean** |
|---|---|
| You don't smoke, do you? | I don't think you do – is that right? |
| Sheila isn't married, is she? | I don't think she is – is that right? |

The sentence *you* use shows what *you* think:

| | |
|---|---|
| Paul's been to London, hasn't he? | The speaker thinks Paul *has*. |
| Paul hasn't been to London, has he? | The speaker thinks Paul *hasn't*. |

You don't just *answer* invitation tags, you add some extra information:

| | |
|---|---|
| You can speak German, can't you. | ▷ Yes, a bit. I learned at school. |
| There's a car park near the theatre, isn't there. | ▷ Yes, in Gifford Street. |
| We haven't got time for a cup to tea, have we. | ▷ No, the train goes at ten to. |

Notice these:

There's a post office in Churchill Road, isn't there.

*There* in the tag too.

You will remember to post that letter, won't you.

The tag for *will* is *won't*.

Let's have a cup of tea, shall we?

The tag for *let's* is *shall we*.

# Asking questions — the basic pattern

| Statement | Question | | |
|---|---|---|---|
| | **Auxiliary** | **Subject** | **Verb** |
| **Sentences with one auxiliary** | | | |
| It was raining. | Was | it | raining? |
| He's seen the doctor. | Has | he | seen the doctor? |
| You can read my writing. | Can | you | read my writing? |
| **Sentences with more than one auxiliary — use the first** | | | |
| She's been waiting a long time. | Has | she | been waiting a long time? |
| They're going to buy a new car. | Are | they | going to buy a new car? |
| **Sentences with no auxiliary — present simple and past simple — use (do)** | | | |
| The bus stops in Salisbury Road. | Does | the bus | stop in Salisbury Road? |
| She caught the plane. | Did | she | catch the plane? |

**Note**
For (be) see page 34; for (have) see page 32.

# Question word questions

John told Mary.    **Who told Mary?**    1. The question is about the *subject* of the sentence.

**Who did John tell?**    2. The question is about the *object* of the sentence. The question is made in the usual way. (See **2.** below)

**1.** Here are some more examples with *who* or *what* as the subject:

**Who** paid?                    **Who** knows about it?
**Who** told you?                **What** happened?
**Who** lives next door?         **What** caused the accident?
**Who** brought Amin to work?

**2.** Most question word questions are made in this way:

| Question word | auxiliary | subject | verb |
|---|---|---|---|
| **How many** | did | you | buy? |
| **How often** | have | you | been there? |
| **How** | can | I | get in touch with you? |
| **Which** | did | you | choose? |
| **When** | will | she | know the results? |
| **Where** | were | they | going? |
| **What** | are | we | going to do about it? |
| **Who** | could | we | ask to help? |
| **Why** | would | you | like to go? |
| | | | |
| **Which floor** | do | you | live on? |
| **Which night** | are | they | going to the cinema? |
| **Whose car** | were· | you | driving yesterday? |
| **Whose book** | did | you | borrow? |

# the . . . ing form (verbal noun)   Your driving makes me nervous.

| | |
|---|---|
| **As subject or object** | **Travelling** makes you tired. |
| | **Listening** to music helps me to relax. |
| | Mike's hobby is **painting.** |

**After:**

| | |
|---|---|
| (do) the | Have you **done the ironing?** |
| go | They usually **go shopping** on Saturday. |
| hate | I **hate getting up** early. |
| love | I **love driving**. |
| enjoy | Do you **enjoy playing** tennis? |
| finish | I'll just **finish writing** this letter. |
| stop (see below) | Jack's **stopped smoking** at last. |
| suggest | Peter **suggested going** to Ibiza. |
| need | My hair **needs washing**. |
| can't help | I **can't help wishing** I hadn't told you. |

**Note**

He stopped smoking. = *He smoked but now he doesn't.*

He stopped to smoke. = *He was doing something but stopped so he could have a cigarette.*

| After: | |
|---|---|
| go on | He **went on complaining** all evening. |
| miss | Do you **miss living** in London? |
| Would you mind . . . | **Would you mind lending** me your pen, please? |
| (be) used to | **I'm not used to driving** in town. |
| afraid of | **I'm afraid of flying.** |
| without | You can't get in **without paying.** |
| It's worth | **It's worth applying** for a grant. |
| It's no use . . . | **It's no use arguing.** |
| It's no good. . . | **It's no good complaining** |
| instead of | We'll drive **instead of catching** the train. |
| What about . . . | **What about having** a picnic? |
| interested in | **I'm not interested in spending** more than £3. |

# Phrasal Verbs

Many verbs in English are made of two, or sometimes three, words. Even if you know the meaning of each word, you cannot guess the meaning of the words together.

**drop**     = *fall* or *let fall*
**drop in** = *visit*

Here is a list of the most common.

| Phrasal verb | Example | Meaning |
|---|---|---|
| break down | The car **broke down** at the weekend. | stop functioning |
| bring up | Children are **brought up** differently in other countries. | educate in the family |
| call back | Could you **call back** tomorrow please? | telephone again |
| call for | **I'll call for** you at 7 o'clock. | collect |
| call off | They**'ve called off** the strike. | cancel |
| carry on | Are you going to **carry on** studying German? | continue |
| catch up | You set off – I'll **catch** you **up.** | hurry after and join |
| close down | The factory **closed down** last year. | close permanently |
| come from | He **comes from** Bangladesh. | was born in |
| drop in | Why not **drop in** on your way home from work? | visit casually |
| eat out | It's nice to **eat out** for a change. | eat in a restaurant |
| fall out | Liz and Jack **have fallen out** again. | quarrel |
| fall through | I'm afraid our holiday plans **have fallen through.** | collapse (plan, arrangement) |
| fill in | Would you **fill in** your name and address please? | complete (a form) |
| find out | I hope nobody **finds out.** | discover the truth |

| Phrasal verb | Example | Meaning |
| --- | --- | --- |
| get back | We **got back** from France last night. | return |
| get off | You **get off** at the end of East Street. | leave the bus |
| get on | How **are** the children **getting on** at school? | succeed |
| get on with | I **get on** very well **with** him. | agree, work well together |
| get out of | I can't **get out of** it. | avoid |
| get over | I had an operation but **I'm getting over** it now. | recover |
| get round to | I **haven't got round to** writing to him yet. | find time to do |
| get through | Did you **get through**? | make a successful phone call |
| get up | I **got up** at 7 this morning. | rise from bed |
| give up | I know it's difficult, but **don't give up!** | stop trying |
| go off | I think the milk**'s gone off.** | become bad (of food) |
| grow up | Children **grow up** more quickly nowadays. | mature |
| hang up | She **hung up** on me! | finish a phone call |
| have on | You**'re having** me **on!** | tease |
| hold on | Can you **hold on** a moment please? | wait, particularly on the phone |
| keep up | How long do you think they can **keep** that **up?** | maintain, continue |
| knock down | She **was knocked down** in First Avenue. | be in a traffic accident |
| laugh at | **Are** you **laughing at** me? | be amused by |
| let down | You **won't let** me **down**, will you? | disappoint |
| lie in | I'm going to **lie in** in the morning. | stay in bed |
| look after | Who**'s looking after** the children? | take care of |

| Phrasal verb | Example | Meaning |
|---|---|---|
| look at | What **are** you **looking at?** | examine carefully |
| look for | They**'re looking for** 20 new staff. | seek |
| look forward to | I**'m** really **looking forward to** my holiday. | anticipate with pleasure |
| look out for | I**'ll look out for** you at the station. | try to meet |
| look up | You can **look** it **up** in the dictionary. | seek information in a book |
| pack up | It's time to **pack up** and go home. | stop |
| pay back | If you lend me it I'll **pay** you **back** tomorrow. | return a debt |
| pay off | He **was paid off** at the end of June. | make redundant |
| pick up | Can I **pick** you **up** at the station? | collect (by car) |
| put off | Shall we **put** it **off** until next week? | delay |
| put off | I hope I**'m** not **putting** you **off.** | distract |
| put on | Don't forget to **put** your coat **on.** | wear |
| put through | Could you **put** me **through** to Mr Wilson please? | connect, on the telephone |
| put up | Can I **put** you **up** for the weekend? | accommodate |
| put up with | I'm afraid you'll just have to **put up with** it. | tolerate |
| ring back | Can you **ring back** please? | re-telephone |
| run out of | We**'ve run out of** sugar. | (there's no . . . left) |
| save up | I**'m saving up** for my holiday. | put aside money |
| see off | Can we **see** you **off** at the airport? | go with to station, airport etc. |
| set off | What time shall we **set off?** | start a journey |
| settle down | My mother thinks I should **settle down.** | establish a regular home |

| Phrasal verb | Example | Meaning |
|---|---|---|
| show off | Stop **showing off!** | boast, look for compliments |
| sleep in | Sorry I'm late – I **slept in.** | wake up late |
| sort out | These files need **sorting out.** | arrange systematically |
| stand up for | You have to **stand up for** what you believe. | defend |
| take after | Carol **takes after** her father. | resemble |
| take off | Would you like to **take** your coat **off?** | remove (clothes) |
| take off | What time do we **take off?** | (for a plane) |
| tell off | I **told** the children **off.** | reprimand |
| think about | What **are** you **thinking about?** | consider |
| think of | You should have **thought of** that earlier. | pay attention to |
| think over | I'd like to **think** it **over** for a while. | consider carefully |
| try on | Could I **try** it **on** please? | check clothes (for size etc) |
| turn down | His application **has been turned down.** | refuse, reject |
| turn off | Would you **turn** the tap **off** please? | stop |
| turn on | Would you **turn** the television **on** please? | switch on |
| turn up | I can't hear it. Can you **turn** it **up** please? | make louder (radio, TV) |
| wake up | What time did you **wake up?** | wake from sleep |
| walk out | The whole work force **walked out.** | go on strike |
| wash up | Who's going to **wash up?** | wash dishes |
| wear out | These shoes **have worn out** very quickly. | become old and unuseable |
| wrap up | Would you like me to **wrap** it **up** for you? | put in paper |

# a, an

**an** in front of a vowel *sound*
in front of **a e i o u**                    in *front of h* when it is not sounded

| **an** | apple | orange |
|---|---|---|
| | egg | uncle |
| | island | |

| **an** | hour | honour |
|---|---|---|

**a** in front of all other letters       in front of **u** and **eu** when it sounds like *you*

| **a** | bag | girl |
|---|---|---|
| | child | house |
| | face | |

| **a** | university | European |
|---|---|---|

She's **a** dentist.                                  With a singular (countable) noun
We had **an** argument.
**A** pound of tomatoes please.

**a** hundred, **a** thousand, **a** million          With certain numbers

**a** dozen, **a** couple of, **a** pair of, **a** lot, **a** few, **a** little    With certain quantities
We spent **a** couple of weeks in Spain.
There were **a** lot of people at the game.

30 pence **a** pound                                  Costs
sixty miles **an** hour                               Measurements

**Note**
*a/an* is normal, *one* is used for emphasis:
      **A:** A coke and two lemonades, please.
      **B:** Two lemonades and two cokes.
      **A:** No, two lemonades and **one** Coke, please.

Only one spelling:      **The** dress, girl, police, children

Two pronunciations:     in front of a consonant sound / ðə /    **the** side
                        in front of a vowel sound      / ð i: /    **the** apple, **the** engine, **the** ice-cream,
                                                                **the** other one, **the** umbrella

|  |  |
|---|---|
|  | **the** is usually used with: |
| I left **the** car in George Street. (= *my* or *our* car) | a person or thing already identified or known |
| Which dress did you buy? ▷ **The** blue one. |  |
| Can you close **the** door please? |  |
| He bought the house next to **the** Post Office. |  |
| **the** China Sea, **the** Ganges, **the** Alps Lake Ontario, Windermere | names of seas, rivers, mountain ranges (but *not* lakes) |
| **the** Taj Mahal, **the** White House **the** Eiffel Tower | important buildings |
| He plays **the** guitar and **the** piano. | musical instruments |

**Note**

1. Most street names do **not** have *the* in front of them: George Street, Queens Road, but *the* High Street.

2. *The* is not used with **at work, at home, at school, go to work, go home, go to school:**
   *He goes to school at eight o'clock. What time does he go home?*

3. *The* is not used with nouns used with a general meaning: *Milk is good for you. I don't like coffee.*

# Countable and uncountable nouns

English nouns are divided into two groups:

## Countable nouns
Are seen by the speaker in *units*

**a glass**

**a cup**

**a glass of water**   **a cup of tea**

**a spoonful of sugar**   **a slice of bread**

## Uncountable nouns
Are **not** seen by the speaker in *units*

**water**   **tea**

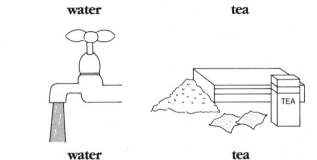

**water**   **tea**

**sugar**   **bread**

## Countable nouns

– have singular and plural forms

– take singular and plural verbs

That **boy is** French.
Those **boys are** French.
The **timetable changes** tomorrow.
The **timetables** all **change** tomorrow.

– can have **a/an** and numbers in front of them

**an** apple          **a** good idea
**four** apples       **three** good ideas

– have **not many** in front of them

He has**n't many** friends.
There were**n't many** people there.

– have **a few** in front of them

Will you have **a few** more cherries?

## Uncountable nouns

– only have one form

– always take a singular verb

**Music helps** me to relax.
Their **furniture is** very modern.
Too much **coffee isn't** good for you.
The **weather was** beautiful all week.

– never have **a/an** or a number *directly* in front

weather        information       advice
furniture      leather

– have **not much** in front of them

He has**n't much** money.
We have**n't** had **much** information yet.

– have **a little** in front of them

Will you have **a little** more ice-cream?

**Note**
*Much* and *many* are used in *negatives* and *questions;* in positive remarks *a lot of* is normally used:

There were **a lot of** people in town today.
We had **a lot of** trouble getting here.

# a . . . of . . .

To make countable quantities with uncountable nouns use *a . . . of . . .*

| a | piece<br>pound<br>pint<br>jar<br>glass<br>tin | of | information<br>tomatoes<br>milk<br>jam<br>water<br>soup | a | packet<br>bit<br>slice<br>litre<br>plate<br>tube | of | cigarettes<br>luck<br>toast<br>oil<br>spaghetti<br>toothpaste |
|---|---|---|---|---|---|---|---|

Some words which are countable in some other languages are uncountable in English:

**advice   information   news   luggage   knowledge   furniture   health**

Some words can be used in two different ways, one countable, one uncountable:

There's *a hair* on your coat.

What *a* lovely *colour!*

Have some more *potatoes.*
▷Just *a few* please.

Her *hair* is beautiful.

Television is very dull without *colour.*

Have some more *potato.*
▷Just *a little* please.

Most nouns make their plural by adding **−s**.
There are three different pronunciations:

| | | | |
|---|---|---|---|
| packet | packets | add /s/ | after a voiceless sound (see p98) |
| hand | hands | add /z/ | after a voiced sound (see p98) |
| face | faces | add /ɪz/ | after these sounds /s/ /z/ / ʃ / /tʃ / /dʒ/ |

Some common plurals are different:

| | | | |
|---|---|---|---|
| woman | **women** | wife | **wives** |
| man | **men** | knife | **knives** |
| child | **children** | foot | **feet** |
| person | **people** | tooth | **teeth** |
| potato | **potatoes** | baby | **babies** |
| bus | **buses** | lady | **ladies** |
| glass | **glasses** | city | **cities** |
| match | **matches** | sheep | **sheep** |

# some, any

**I bought some fruit. Anybody upstairs can help you.**

**some** is about *part*, or *not all*; **any** is about *all* or *none*.

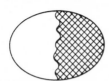

I like **some** fruit.

I like **any** fruit.

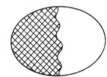

I don't like **some** fruit.

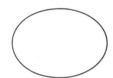

I don't like **any** fruit.

## any

She doesn't drink **any** alcohol, not even beer.    None

There aren't **any** shops near our flat.

You can take **any** bus from the station.    All

When can you come round?
▷ **Any** day next week.

I like **any** kind of cheese.

Did you take **any** photographs?    "Open" questions

Have you **any** small change, please?

## some

**Some** of the trains stop here but some don't.

**Some** people thought it was too expensive.

I like **some** pop music, but not all.

*Not all*

I've bought **some** tea but we need **some** sugar.

Would you like us to bring **some** sandwiches with us?

I'd like **some** information about flights to Paris please.

*General quantity*

These words are used in the same way:

| | | | |
|---|---|---|---|
| **somebody** | **someone** | **something** | **somewhere** |
| **anybody** | **anyone** | **anything** | **anywhere** |

There's **somebody** outside to see you.

We can go **anywhere** with this ticket.

There's **something** wrong with my arm.

I don't think there's **anything** we can do about it.

Let's go **somewhere** warm this year!

I've never been **anywhere** in Scotland except Glasgow.

These two questions are similar in meaning:

Can I get you **something** to eat?

Can I get you **anything** to eat?

*any* suggests an **open** question: *I don't know if you would like a sandwich or not.*

*some* suggests a **restricted** question: *You must be hungry. I suppose you are ready to eat.*

# Adjectives

My wallet is **black**.

I've lost a **black** wallet.

I've lost a **black leather** wallet.

Adjectives give more information about a noun.

The boy was **late.**

The girls were **late,** too.

Singular and plural are the same.

She's a **really nice** person.

It's **very cheap.**

Use *very* or *really* to make an adjective stronger.

| | | Comparative | Superlative |
|---|---|---|---|
| **Short adjectives** | | | |
| one syllable | **cheap** | **cheaper** | **the cheapest** |
| two syllables ending in -y | **early** | **earlier** | **the earliest** |
| **Long adjectives** | | | |
| two syllables | **careful** | **more careful** | **the most careful** |
| more syllables | **difficult** | **more difficult** | **the most difficult** |
| **Irregular adjectives** | | | |
| | **good** | **better** | **the best** |
| | **bad** | **worse** | **the worst** |

# Comparison of Adjectives

Ahmed is **older than** Razi.

The book is **better than** the film.

This baker is **more expensive than** the one round the corner.

Have you any **smaller** oranges?

Have you anything a bit **cheaper?**

I think yours is **better.**

Comparative + *than*

Maria is **as old as** Marco.

Gas isn't **as expensive as** electricity.

Was he **as angry as** he looked?

*as* + adjective + *as*

## Superlatives

Razi is **the tallest** in the class.

Gabi is **the most careful** driver I know.

How much is **the cheapest** flight to Athens?

The **most expensive** isn't always **the best.**

Where's **the nearest** toilet, please?

*the* + superlative

# Adverbs

## Regular

| Adjective | | Adverb | |
|---|---|---|---|
| slow | careful | slowly | carefully |
| easy | sensible | easily | sensibly |

He's a slow reader.
It's easy to make it yourself.

He reads slowly.          + -ly
You can easily make it yourself.     -y →ily

## Irregular

Adjective and adverb the same:

| | | |
|---|---|---|
| hard | late | early |
| fast | straight | |
| harder | earlier | faster |

**Adjective**

He has long **straight** hair.
Let's catch the **late** train.
She's a **hard** worker.
Is there an **earlier** train?
The train is **faster,** but more expensive.

**Adverb**

Go **straight** along Cromwell Road . . . .
The train arrived 10 minutes **late.**
She works **hard.**
Can you come to me **earlier** than 10, please?
I wish I could read **faster.**

# Special adverbs

| | Adjective | Adverb | |
|---|---|---|---|
| They're a good team. | good | well | They played well last Saturday. |
| These are a better buy. | better | better | Do you feel better now? |

These words look like adverbs formed in the usual way but have special meanings:

| | | | |
|---|---|---|---|
| **nearly** | = almost | | Be careful! You **nearly** spilt your tea. |
| **hardly** (any) | = almost none | | There's **hardly** any butter left. |
| **lately** | = in the near past | | I haven't seen her **lately**. |
| **shortly** | = in the near future | | I'll have to be going home **shortly**. |
| **directly** | = immediately | | I'll let you know **directly** I hear myself. |

## Making adverbs stronger

carefully    **more carefully**    **much more carefully**    **as carefully as possible**

You must do your homework **carefully**.  → You'll have to do it again **much more carefully**.
Please tell him **soon**.  → Please tell him **as soon as possible**.

## Comparing adjectives or adverbs

The same structures are used for comparing adjectives or adverbs:

| Comparative + than | Ahmed is **older than** Razi. |
|---|---|
| | This restaurant is **more expensive than** that one. |
| | She speaks English **more confidently than** her brother. |
| | Liverpool played **better than** they did last week. |
| Not as . . . as | Razi isn't **as old as** Ahmed. |
| | Chinese food isn't **as interesting as** Indian. |
| | He doesn't speak English **as confidently as** his sister. |
| | Liverpool didn't play **as well as** they did last week. |

# Position of adverbs

The rules are very complicated. Here are some useful tips:

**1.** If you are unsure, put the adverb *at the end* of the sentence.

**2.** These adverbs of time usually come after **(be)** or after the first auxiliary.

| | |
|---|---|
| **always, often,**<br>**usually, sometimes,**<br>**never, already** | Peter is **never** late.<br>You must **always** lock the door.<br>We've **sometimes** had lunch at work. |

**3.** These adverbs make an adjective or adverb stronger or weaker.
They come *in front of* the adjective or adverb.

| | |
|---|---|
| **very, too, so,**<br>**rather, really, quite,**<br>**extremely, slightly** | Richard can swim **very well.**<br>It's **too far** to walk.<br>It was **quite cold** in the water.<br>This is a bad line – it's **extremely difficult** to hear you. |

**4. ever**     mainly in questions     Have you **ever** been to Manchester?

**5. enough**     *after* an adjective     He isn't **strong enough.**
or adverb     He didn't work **hard enough.**
*in front of* a noun     I haven't **enough money.**

# Personal pronouns

| Subject pronoun | Object pronoun | Possessive adjective | Possessive pronoun | Reflexive pronoun |
|---|---|---|---|---|
| I | me | my | mine | myself |
| you | you | your | yours | yourself |
| we | us | our | ours | ourselves |
| they | them | their | theirs | themselves |
| he | him | his | his | himself |
| she | her | her | hers | herself |
| it | it | its | its | itself |

Use a pronoun instead of a noun when it is clear *who* or *what* you are talking about.

**Object pronouns**

Would you like to come with **us?**

Do you live near **them?**

Could you send them direct to **me**, please?

*after a preposition*

Who broke that window?
▷ It wasn't **me**.

*after (**be**) instead of a subject pronoun*

Can Eva send them to **me,** please?

Tony made it for **her.**

*After to and for with make, give, send, lend, pass, take, show*

**Note**

*Yourself* is for one person; *yourselves* is for more than one person.

# Possessives

## Adjective

Tells you who owns something

**My** feet hurt!
*Is this* **your** sweater?
I don't think this is **his** car, is it?
Sheila's left **her** bag somewhere in here.
**Our** children like **their** school.
What's **your** phone number?

## Pronoun

Instead of a possessive adjective and a noun

▷ So do **mine!** = *So do my feet*
▷ Yes, where's **yours?**
▷ No, **his** is over there.
▷ I think this is **hers,** isn't it?
▷ Yes, **ours** like **theirs**, too.
▷ 7726981. What's **yours?**

## Reflexive pronouns

He's cut **himself.**

Oh dear! Have you hurt **yourself?**

The subject and the object are the same.

Did you do the decorations **yourself?**
▷ I did the painting **myself,** but that's all.

Used for emphasis

Can I give you a hand?
▷ No, it's all right thanks. I can do it **myself.**

## Some special expressions

| Help | |
|------|--------------|
| Enjoy | **yourself!** |
| Behave | **yourselves!** |

I live **by myself.** = I live *on my own.*
He lives **by himself.** = He lives *on his own.*
They live **by themselves.** = They live *on their own.*

**They** is used to talk about:

> **1.** more than one person: *The children are excited – they're going on a trip tomorrow.*

> **2.** a general group of people:

| | |
|---|---|
| **They** are repairing the road. | *they* = the Town Council |
| **They** want to increase income tax. | *they* = the Government |
| **They** say it's a marvellous film. | *they* = a lot of people |
| **They** tell me you are changing your job. | *they* = somebody or some people |

**They** and **their** are also used to talk about *one* person with:

| | |
|---|---|
| some- | |
| any- | -body |
| no- | -one |
| every- | |

**Someone** has left **their** pen on the desk.

**Somebody** told you, didn't **they!**

**Anybody** knows that, don't **they!**

**Everyone** has to bring **their** own food.

If **anyone** rings while I'm out, please ask **them** to ring back.

# it

it is used as a pronoun in the usual way: *There is a car park but it's full at the moment.*

it is also used for:

| | | |
|---|---|---|
| Weather | **It's** raining. | **It** was snowing. |
| | **It's** rather cold. | **It** was a very warm evening. |
| Time | **It's** three o'clock. | **It's** the fifth today, isn't it. |
| | **It's** getting late. | **It's** time to go. |
| | **It's** a long time ago. | **It's** Saturday tomorrow. |
| Distance | **It's** about two miles. | **It's** not far. |
| | How far is **it** to Oxford? | **It's** rather a long way. |

It is also used as a dummy subject when *is ('s)* is followed by certain adjectives:

**It's essential to** be there by 7 o'clock.

**It's difficult to** believe that.

**It's possible to** get a bus.

**It's interesting to** see new places.

**It's lovely to** have a day off.

**It's not true that** he's changing his job.

**It's best to** get a taxi.

**It's better to** phone her.

**Note**

**It's no use** ask**ing** Peter – he wasn't there.

**It's worth** ask**ing** him – he might know.

That train is too early. What time is the next (~~train~~) **one.**
The French apples are 50p, but the English (~~apples~~) **ones** are only 45p.

*Use one or ones instead of repeating the same noun.*

| the<br>this/that | one |
|---|---|
| which | one? |

| the<br>these/those | ones |
|---|---|
| which | ones? |

I'm going to make a cup of coffee. Would you like **one?**
▷ Mm yes, I'd love **one,** thank you.

Which is your bike?
▷ **The** blue **one, the one** next to the car.

Shall I use these tea-bags?
▷ No, use **the ones** on the shelf, please.

**Which one** do you prefer?
▷ **That one's** lovely, but I think **this one** will suit me better.

# there + (be)

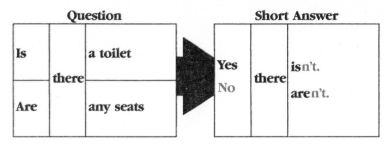

| There | 's isn't | a problem |
|---|---|---|
| | aren't | six |

**Question**

| Is | | a toilet |
|---|---|---|
| | there | |
| Are | | any seats |

**Short Answer**

| Yes | | isn't. |
|---|---|---|
| No | there | aren't. |

**There's** a cinema in the centre.

**Is there** a telephone box in the station?

**There are** some people waiting outside.

**Are there** 2 m's in 'recommend'?

**There's** nothing we can do about it.

**There's** somebody waiting for you outside.

**Is there** anywhere to eat near here?

When you talk about something for the first time

**There must be** a mistake.

**There might be** a strike.

**There can be** a lot of rain at this time of year.

**There should be** a bus in five minutes.

**There'll be** trouble when he finds out!

With an auxiliary and *be*

**There** isn't enough room, **is there?**
▷ Oh yes, I think **there is.**

*There* is repeated in the tag and in the short answer.

| this | these |
|------|-------|
| → o | → 88 o |
| that | those |
| → o | → 88 o |

Use:
1. in front of a noun
2. alone when it is clear what you are talking about

Does **this** bus go to Victoria, please?
Does **this** go to Victoria please?

**These** strawberries are delicious.
**These** are delicious.

Things that are physically near.

**This** is the life!

**These** science fiction films are a waste of money.

Things which are "psychologically near"; the speaker feels they are near at the moment of speaking.

How much is **that** dress please?
How much is **that** please?

A pound of **those** tomatoes please.
A pound of **those** please.

Things which are physically remote.

**That** was lucky! I didn't expect **that.**

**That** kind of person really annoys me.

Is **that** all?

Things which are "psychologically remote" from the speaker at the moment of speaking.

# that, who, which

**The car that was parked outside has gone.**

**that, who** and **which** introduce more information about a person, thing, or idea.

The woman **that** lives next door is very friendly.
Could I speak to the doctor **that** I saw yesterday, please?
The essay **that** won the prize was written by a German student.

*Tells us which woman.*
*Tells us which doctor.*
*Tells us which essay.*

The person **who** told me had been there himself.

It was the blue car **which** caused the accident.

The thing **that** really surprised me was the price.

*Often used with the thing that . . .*

The thing **that** I really enjoyed was the music.

*That* is usual in spoken English.

In written English use: *who* with people        *which* with things.

*that, who, which* are usually left out if they are the object of the verb that follows.

The man **who** I saw yesterday told me to come at ten o'clock.
→ **The man I saw yesterday told me to come at ten o'clock.**

Can I collect the coat **that** I brought in last week, please?
→ **Can I collect the coat I brought in last week, please?**

| | | |
|---|---|---|
| **about** | the subject of a conversation idea, book, etc. | Tell me **about** your family. What are you thinking **about?** |
| **at** | certain special expressions | **At** home, **at** school, **at** work, **at** university, **at** the cinema, **at** the end of . . . . |
| **by** | the person or thing that did something | It was written **by** William Golding. I was shocked **by** what she told me. |
| | transport | We went **by** train. |
| **for** | purpose + noun or . . . *ing* form | Let's go **for** a cup of coffee. This machine's **for** peeling potatoes. |
| | a general period of time | We were there **for** three weeks. I haven't seen you **for** ages. |
| **from** | place of origin | Where is he **from?** They come **from** Sri Lanka. |
| **with** | in company | Would you like to come **with** us? |
| | what you use to do something | He cut himself **with** his pen-knife. |

# Prepositions — Time

**On**
| | |
|---|---|
| **Friday** | Day |
| **Wednesday morning** | Day + *morning, afternoon,* |
| **Wednesday night** | *evening, night* |
| **the sixteenth of March** | Date |
| **Christmas Day** | Special Day |

**At**
| | |
|---|---|
| **two o'clock** | Time |
| **Christmas** | Festival |
| **lunchtime** | Mealtimes |
| **the weekend** | |
| **night** | |

**In**
| | |
|---|---|
| **Spring** | Season |
| **1947** | Year |
| **August** | Month |
| **the morning** | |
| **the evening** | |

Sometimes *during* and *in* have the same meaning: *in the night* is very unusual; *during the night* is normal.

## Periods

| | |
|---|---|
| **For three weeks** | General period |
| **In three weeks** | Period starting from now |
| **Three weeks ago** | Period ending now |

**Note**
*ago* goes *after* the period.

Sometimes we talk about a *point*

a *period*   between two points

**at** 2 o'clock

We arrived **at** 2 o'clock.

**before** 2 o'clock

The doctor can't see you **before** 2 o'clock.

**until** 2 o'clock = not before 2

I won't be there **until** 2 o'clock.

**since** 2 o'clock

I haven't seen her **since** 2 o'clock.

(looking back to a point in the past,
with a perfect form of the verb.)

**about** 2 o'clock

We'll be there **about** 2 o'clock.

**after** 2 o'clock

I'll be in my office **after** 2 o'clock.

**by** 2 o'clock = *any* point *before* or *at* 2

or

Will we be there **by** 2 o'clock?

**from** 2 o'clock

They are open **from** 2 o'clock.

# Prepositions — Where?

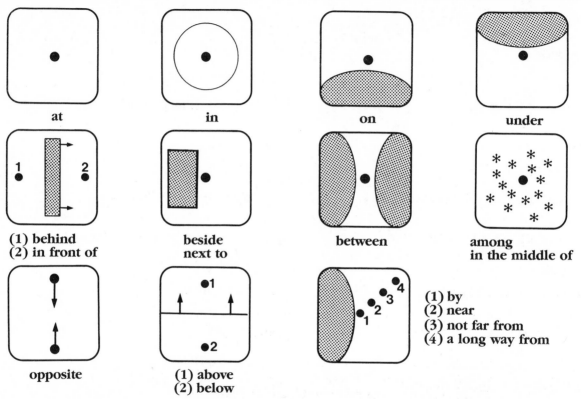

at

in

on

under

(1) behind
(2) in front of

beside
next to

between

among
in the middle of

opposite

(1) above
(2) below

(1) by
(2) near
(3) not far from
(4) a long way from

**Note**
To talk about a building: *David's inside. He's gone inside.*

**at**
He lives **at** number five.
Turn left **at** the top of the stairs.
I'll meet you **at** the station.

at an exact place

**in**
We live **in** England.
Kyoko works **in** Birmingham.
He lives **in** Baker Street.
Were you **in** the pub last night?
Throw it **in** the wastepaper bin!

a country
a town
a street
a building or area
a container

**on**
I'll meet you **on** the platform.
There's some coffee **on** the shelf.

| | |
|---|---|
| under | She hid the letter **under** her book. |
| in front of | I'll see you **in front of** the Town Hall. |
| behind | Grace Road is **behind** the bus station. |
| next to | We live **next to** the post office. |
| beside | Can I sit **beside** you? |
| between | We live **between** Queen's Road and the sea. |
| in the middle of | The bus station is **in the middle of** town. |
| among | I found this scarf **among** some old clothes. |
| opposite | There's a bus stop directly **opposite** the entrance. |
| above | Our flat is **above** the bakers. |
| below | The bakers is **below** our flat. |
| by | I'll be standing **by** the ticket office. |
| near | Is there a bank **near** the station? |
| not far from | I walk to college because it's **not far from** home. |
| a long way from | We live **a long way from** the shops. |

# Prepositions — Where to?

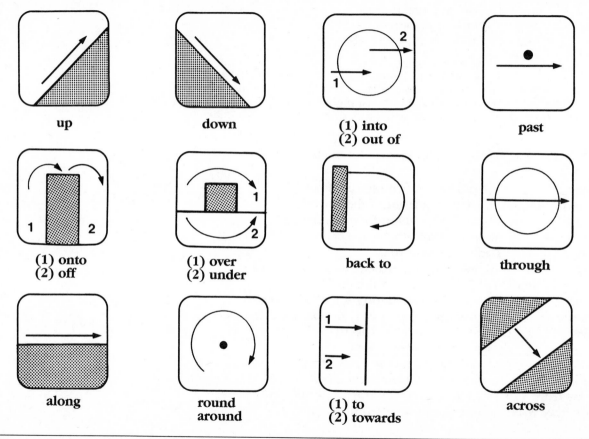

up

down

(1) into
(2) out of

past

(1) onto
(2) off

(1) over
(2) under

back to

through

along

round
around

(1) to
(2) towards

across

| | |
|---|---|
| up | Go **up** this road then turn left. |
| down | Karen fell **down** the stairs. |
| into | I saw him getting **into** a taxi. |
| out of | Can you get the eggs **out of** the fridge, please. |
| past | He walked straight **past** me without speaking. |
| onto | The cat jumped **onto** her knee. |
| off | It fell **off** the table and broke. |
| round | I'm tired – I've walked **round** town today. |
| back to | Can we go **back to** the theatre please – I've forgotten my coat. |
| through | I hate driving **through** the town at this time of day. |
| aiong | They walked **along** the beach. |
| over | I tripped **over** a stone on the pavement. |
| under | The cat ran **under** the car. |
| to | They rushed **to** the door. |
| across | He ran **across** the road. |

# Conjunctions

A conjunction joins two ideas:

| | | | |
|---|---|---|---|
| **A:** | Tea **or** coffee? | **or** | joins alternatives |
| **B:** | Tea, please. | | |
| **A:** | Sugar **and** milk? | **and** | joins two *similar* ideas |
| **B:** | Milk **but** no sugar, thank you. | **but** | joins two *different* or *opposite* ideas |

**or, and, but**  1. come between the ideas they join.
2. can join two sentences.

You can change it.
You can have your money back.  →You can change it **or** you can have your money back.

The surgery opens at 9.00
The surgery closes at 12.00  → The surgery opens at 9.00 **and** closes at 12.00

I'd love to come.
I'm busy on Saturday.  → I'd love to come **but** I'm busy on Saturday.

**so** gives the *result* of the first part of the sentence. It is the second part of the sentence.

The class was boring, **so** I left.        The rent is too high, **so** we are moving.

**so that** gives the *purpose* for something. It is usually the second part of the sentence.

I need a nursery place **so that** I can go to work.

You'd better write it down **so that** you don't forget.

With these words the two parts of the sentence can come in either order with the same meaning:

**Because** we were late, we took a taxi.    **If** she comes, I'll tell her.
We took a taxi **because** we were late.    I'll tell her, **if** she comes.

**if** gives the *condition* for the other part of the sentence to be true.

I'll do it **if** you'll help me.

She's going to change her job **if** she can.

**If** anyone rings, can you ask them to call back, please?

**although** *contrasts* two ideas.

**Although** he's got good qualifications, he can't get a job.

I'm going to get one, **although** they are very expensive.

**because** gives the *reason* for something; answers the question *Why?*

**Because** we were late, we took a taxi.

I didn't come **because** it was raining.

These words show the *connection in time;* answer the question *When?*

| | |
|---|---|
| **as** | The lorry hit us **as** we were turning the corner. |
| **when** | I'll tell her **when** I see her. |
| **while** | They arrived **while** we were trying to phone them! |
| **since** | Where have you been living **since** you came to England? |
| **till/until** | Could you keep an eye on things **until** I get back, please? |
| **before** | I hope he gets here **before** the train leaves. |
| **after** | I'll see you here **after** I've been to the bank. |
| **as soon as** | Phone us **as soon as** your plane gets in. |

# If

If can be used with many different structures. Here are the most common.
It is usually possible to have the *if* part of the sentence as the first or the second half of the sentence:

**If** Sara's late, she never apologises.
Sara never apologises **if** she's late.

**If** she worked harder, she'd pass.
She'd pass **if** she worked harder.

**General conditions**

| Present simple | | Present simple |
|---|---|---|
| Sara never apologises | | she is late. |
| He gets angry | **if** | you argue with him. |
| How long does milk keep | | you haven't got a fridge? |

**Likely conditions:** things which are very likely to happen.

| 'll (will) | | Present simple |
|---|---|---|
| The doctor'll see you | | you come at nine. |
| I'll ask Ali | **if** | I see him. |
| We'll miss the bus | | we don't hurry. |
| They won't come | | the weather's bad. |

**Unlikely conditions:** things which might happen, but probably not.

| 'd (would) | | Past simple |
|---|---|---|
| She'd pass | **if** | she worked harder. |
| He wouldn't be happy | | he lived on his own. |

## Impossible conditions

| 'd have + third form | | Past perfect (had + third form) |
|---|---|---|
| I'd have told you<br>We'd have been there on time | **if** | I had known myself.<br>we'd caught the earlier bus. |

## Instructions, advice

| Imperative | | Present simple |
|---|---|---|
| Stay in bed tomorrow<br>Get the early train | **if** | you don't feel better.<br>you want to get there in time. |

If can also join sentences with a modal auxiliary. Here are some examples:

What should I do **if** the baby cries?

Can I see the manager **if** I come back later?

May I leave **if** I finish the job before five o'clock?

You ought to go to the doctor **if** it doesn't get better soon.


## Note

The use of the sentence with *if* is the same as the sentence without *if*. The part of the sentence which begins with *if* gives details of the *special situation* the speaker is talking about.

# Numbers

| | | | |
|---|---|---|---|
| 1 | one | first | |
| 2 | two | second | |
| 3 | three | third | |
| 4 | four | fourth | |
| 5 | five | fifth | |
| 6 | six | sixth | |
| 7 | seven | seventh | |
| 8 | eight | eighth | |
| 9 | nine | ninth | |
| 10 | ten | tenth | |
| 11 | eleven | eleventh | |
| 12 | twelve | twelfth | |
| 13 | thirteen | thirteenth | |
| 14 | fourteen | fourteenth | |
| 15 | fifteen | fifteenth | |
| 16 | sixteen | sixteenth | |
| 17 | seventeen | seventeenth | |
| 18 | eighteen | eighteenth | |
| 19 | nineteen | nineteenth | |
| 20 | twenty | twentieth | |
| 21 | twenty-one | twenty-first | |
| 22 | twenty-two | twenty-second | |

| | | |
|---|---|---|
| 30 | thirty | thirtieth |
| 40 | forty | fortieth |
| 50 | fifty | fiftieth |
| 60 | sixty | sixtieth |
| 70 | seventy | seventieth |
| 80 | eighty | eightieth |
| 90 | ninety | ninetieth |
| 100 | a hundred | hundreth |
| 200 | two hundred | two hundredth |
| 1000 | a thousand | thousandth |
| 1,000,000 | a million | millionth |

| Write | Say | | Say | Write |
|---|---|---|---|---|
| $\frac{1}{2}$ | a half | | point five | .5 |
| $\frac{1}{4}$ | a quarter | | point two five | .25 |
| $\frac{3}{4}$ | three quarters | | point seven five | .75 |
| $1\frac{1}{2}$ | one and a half | | | |
| $\frac{1}{6}$ | one sixth | | three point two | 3.2 |

**Have you the time, please?**

**What time is it, please?**
▷ **It's twenty-five to seven.**

**It's**
| exactly |
| just | **three o'clock.**
| about |
| nearly |

**What time does it start?**

**What time does the York train leave, please?**

**The train leaves at six forty-seven.**

**There's a train at fifteen forty.**

**I'll see you about sixish.**
*-ish* gives an approximate time.

o'clock
five to · five past
ten to · ten past
a quarter to · a quarter past
twenty to · twenty past
twenty-five to · twenty-five past
half past

11 12 1
10 · 2
9 · 3
8 · 4
7 6 5

## Days
Monday
Tuesday
Wednesday
Thursday
Friday
Saturday
Sunday

## Seasons
Spring
Summer
Autumn
Winter

## Months
| | |
|---|---|
| January | July |
| February | August |
| March | September |
| April | October |
| May | November |
| June | December |

## Write:
15th July
21.4.54

## Say:
the fifteenth of July
the twenty-first of April, nineteen fifty-four.

# Some Expressions of Time

A long time ago
 Six or seven years ago
  A few years ago
   A couple of years ago
    Eighteen months ago
     Last year
      A few months/weeks ago
       Recently
        The other week
         Last week
          A few days ago
           The other day
            The day before yesterday
             Yesterday
              Yesterday evening
               Last night

Now

Now

In the morning
 Tomorrow morning
  Tomorrow
   The day after tomorrow
    In a day or two
     In a couple of days
      Next Saturday
       Next Sunday evening
        In a few days time
         Soon
          Next week
           A week on Thursday
            Next month
             In a few weeks time
              Next year
               In a couple of years

Future

## At the beginning of a word

| | | |
|---|---|---|
| **un-** | the opposite of | *unmarried* |
| **non-** | not | *non-smoker* |
| **anti-** | against | *anti-American* |
| **pro-** | in favour of | *pro-American* |
| **pre-** | before | *pre-war* |
| **post-** | after | *post-1960* |
| **ex-** | former | *ex-President* |
| **re-** | do again | *re-start* |
| **mis-** | wrongly | *mis-understand* |
| **over-** | too much | *over-confident* |

## At the end of a word

| | | |
|---|---|---|
| **-ness** | adjective → noun | *darkness* |
| **-able** | verb → adjective | *washable* |
| **-en** | adjective → verb | *brighten* |
| **-less** | without | *homeless* |
| **-ful** | a quantity | *cupful* |
| **-ish** | approximately | *youngish* |

# Some pronunciation rules

There are two kinds of consonant sound in English:

**Voiced**
You can feel vibration

**Voiceless**
You can feel no vibration

All vowel sounds are voiced.

These are pairs:

| **Voiced sounds:** | /b/ bin | /v/ view | / ð / with | /d/ said | /z/ zoo | / ʒ / television | / dʒ / bridge | /g/ go |
|---|---|---|---|---|---|---|---|---|
| **Voiceless sounds:** | /p/ pin | /f/ few | / θ / think | /t/ set | /s/ say | / ʃ / fish | / tʃ / church | /k/ come |

| **These are voiced:** | /m/ men | /n/ now | / ŋ / sing | /l/ long | /r/ red |
|---|---|---|---|---|---|

There are three other sounds: /h/, house; /j/ yellow; /w/ wear, but these never come at the end of words.

## Past simple (second form)

The past simple is usually made by adding **-ed.**
There are three pronunciations:

| | | |
|---|---|---|
| /t/ | after a voiceless sound: | *walked* |
| /d/ | after a voiced sound: | *opened* |
| /id/ | after a /t/ or /d/ sound: | *waited* |

## Third person -s

The third person present simple is made by adding **-s.**
There are three pronunciations:

**1.** /s/ after a voiceless sound (except those in 3)    *waits*
**2.** /z/ after a voiced sound (except those in 3)    *opens*
**3.** /iz/ after these sounds /s/, /z/, / ʃ /, / tʃ /, /dʒ/    *passes, loses, washes, watches, judges*

## Plurals

Plurals are usually made by adding **-s.**
Use the same pronunciation rules as for third person-**s.**

**1.** voiceless: /s/    *books, cups*
**2.** voiced: /z/    *games, boys*
**3.** special sounds: /iz/    *buses, houses, wishes, watches, wages*

# Some writing rules

## Possession ('s or s')

| | | |
|---|---|---|
| **'s** | singular | **Ravi's** car is a Ford. |
| | | Whose bag is that?<br>▷ It's **Jean's.** |
| **'s** | irreglar plural nouns | The **children's** room is on the left. |
| **s'** | regular plural nouns | The **boys'** room is at the top of the stairs. |
| | | The **students'** work wasn't very good. |

## Spelling

| | | | | | |
|---|---|---|---|---|---|
| **-ch -sh** | add **e** | before **-s** | watch | → | wat**ches** |
| **-x -s -o** | | | box | → | bo**xes** |
| | | | tomato | → | tomat**oes** |
| **-e** | ~~e~~ | before **-ed** | like | → | lik**ed** |
| | | **-es** | bake | → | bak**es** |
| | | **-est** | late | → | lat**est** |
| **-y** | y→ie | before **-s** | fly | → | **flies** |
| | y→i | before **-ed** | try | → | **tried** |
| | | **-er** | easy | → | eas**ier** |
| | | **-est** | lazy | → | laz**iest** |
| | | **-ly** | happy | → | happ**ily** |
| **Short vowel** | **double** | before **-er** | begin | → | begi**nner** |
| **+ consonant** | **letter** | **-est** | big | → | bi**ggest** |
| | | **-ing** | stop | → | sto**pping** |
| | | **-ed** | permit | → | permi**tted** |

## Advising

**I'd** complain **if I were you.**
**You ought to** take a couple of days off.

*ought to* suggests a stronger, more objective opinion.

## Agreeing

I'm looking forward to the weekend.
▷ **So am I.**

Repeat the same auxiliary in the answer

I love chocolate.
▷**So do I.**

No auxiliary, use **(do)** in the answer

I don't like football on television.
▷ **Neither do I.**

Use *neither* to agree with a negative remark

## Apologising

**I'm sorry.**
▷ **I'm sorry.**

Not really anyone's fault
– *both* say the same

**I AM sorry.**
▷ That's quite all right.

Stress on **am** – a real apology

**Excuse me,** could you change a pound please?

*Excuse me* before you disturb a stranger

**Excuse me,** please.

You want to pass someone

Have you got the tickets yet?
▷ **I'm afraid not.**

Use *I'm afraid* to 'soften' a negative or unhelpful
answer

Could I speak to John please?
▷ **I'm afraid** he's out at the moment.

# Basic Functions

## Asking for something

A pound of apples, **please.**
Could you pass the salt, **please.**

These sound unfriendly without *please*

## Asking someone to do something

Could you spell it, **please.**
**Will you** ask him to ring me, **please.**

Always *please* at the end

**Would you mind** opening the door, **please.**

*Would you mind . . . ing* for people you don't know

## Asking for permission

**May I** borrow your pen?

Personal

**Do you mind if I** smoke?
▷ I'd rather you didn't.

**Is it all right if** I park here?
▷ No, I'm afraid parking isn't allowed.

More objective

## Complaining

I **HAVE** been waiting twenty minutes.
It **WAS** only yesterday I bought it.
You **DID** promise to help me.

Stress the auxiliary to show you are annoyed

## Correcting

I **think you've made a mistake.**
I **think it should be** £2.80, not £3.80.

Usually with *I think*

I **think** it was 1982, **wasn't it?**
I **think** the train goes at ten past, **doesn't it.**

Often with a tag (see page 52)

## Inviting

**Would you like to** have lunch with us?
▷ Oh thank you. I'd love to.
That's very kind of you, but I'm afraid I can't.

## Offering

**Would you like** a cake?                           Offering something
▷ Thank you. I'd love one.

**Let me** carry that for you.                        Offering help
**We'll** do the washing up.
**Shall we** pick you up at the station?

**Can I** give you a hand?                            General offer to help
▷ Thank you. That's very kind of you.
It's all right thank you. I can manage.

**Have** a cake!                                      Use the first form of the verb
**Help** yourself.

## Refusing to do something

I **won't** work on that machine. It's dangerous.
He **won't** tell me.

## Suggesting

**Why don't** you get a taxi?                         To the other person
**You could** send it air mail.

**Let's** go now or we'll be late.                    Doing something *together*
**Let's** go on Saturday evening.
**Why don't we** buy her a pen?

# Basic Functions

## Sympathising

**Oh dear. What a nuisance**
**Oh dear. I AM sorry to hear that.**

Something not very important
More serious. Stress **am.**

## Thanking

**Thank you.**
**Thanks very much.**

Not important

**Thank you.** That **IS** kind of you.
**Thank you.** That makes things **MUCH** easier.
**Thank you.** That **WILL** be a help.

When you are grateful stress one word strongly

## Warning

**Be careful!**
**Look out!**

General

**Mind** the floor, it's slippery.
**Don't forget to** take a coat.

# Useful phrases

## Checking English

Could you say that again, please?
What does this mean, please?
I don't understand this.
How do you spell . . . ?
How do you pronounce this, please?
Is this correct, please?

## Directions in the street

Excuse me, could you tell me where . . . is, please?
Excuse me, is there a . . . near here, please?
Turn left/right.
Take the (second) turning on the left/right.
It's on the left/right.
It's straight ahead.
Go straight along/down/up here.
It's on the corner of Brook Street and Park Lane.

## Asking the time

Have you the time please?
What time do you make it, please?

## When someone is going away

Have a good holiday.
Have a good trip.
Have a safe journey.

## Introducing yourself

I don't think we've met before. I'm *(David Jones)*.

## On the phone

May I speak to . . . please?
▷ Speaking.
Just a moment, please.
Can I take a message?
I'll ask him/her to ring you.
Sorry. I've got the wrong number.

## Sending a greeting to someone

Give my regards to . . .
Remember me to . . .

## On someone's birthday

Many happy returns.
Happy birthday.

## On (or just after) January 1st.

Happy New Year.
▷ Thank you. The same to you.

## Someone has passed an exam, got a job, won something

Congratulations!

## When someone gets engaged

Congratulations. I hope you'll be very happy.

# Time and verb forms

## Time

| PAST<br>Before Now | PRESENT<br>Now | FUTURE<br>After Now |
|---|---|---|

Verbs change their form: I *know* her; I *knew* her.

Some changes are connected with time:

| **Present Tense** | I *know* her. | I *'m waiting* for Jack. | **Present time.** |
| **Past Tense** | I *knew* her. | I *was waiting* for Jack. | **Past time.** |

English verb forms do **not** always correspond directly to time.

| **Present Tense** | I *'m playing* tennis on Saturday. | **Future time.** |
| **Past Tense** | If he *came,* I'd be surprised. | **Future time.** |
| **Present Tense** | Wood *floats* on water | **All times - always true.** |

The difference between verb forms is only *partly* decided by time.
Sometimes other reasons are important too.

The verb form is sometimes decided by the speaker's viewpoint or attitude.

The most important divisions in English are:

**1.** Is the event or action *immediate* or *remote* for the speaker?

    **a.** If it is immediate the speaker uses a *present* form.

    **b.** If it is remote the speaker uses a *past* form.

The "remoteness" may be of different kinds:

| | |
|---|---|
| Remote *in time* | I *went* to school in Leeds. |
| Remote *relationship* | What name *was* it, please? |
| Remote *possibility* | If I *saw* him, I'd tell him. |

**2.** Does the speaker wish to emphasise the event as a *period,* existing between *two* points in time?

    **a.** If the speaker does not want to emphasise an event as a period, a **simple** form is used.

    **b.** If the speaker wants to emphasise the event as a period, a **continuous** form is used.

This is not a matter of *fact.* It depends on how the speaker sees the situation.

All of the following are possible:
Jane *was reading* while Peter *watched* television.
Jane *read* while Peter *watched* television.
Jane *was reading* while Peter *was watching* television.
Jane *read* while Peter *was watching* television.

**3.** In English the speaker can look *back* in time or *forward* in time.

| | | |
|---|---|---|
| Looking *back* in time | He'*d left* before we arrived. | **(have)** + third form |
| Looking *forward* in time | It'*s going to rain.* | **(be) going to** |

## Present simple and Present continuous

The present continuous always refers to an action which the speaker sees as:

**a.** a *period*
**b.** a *limited* period

I usually *drive* to work, but I *'m walking* while the weather is so nice.

The present simple refers to an action which the speaker does **not** see as a limited period. It can be:

**a.** a point
**b.** an *unlimited* period.
**c.** something *always* true.
**d.** a general statement.

I *promise* I won't tell anyone.
Where do you *come* from?
Water *boils* at 100°C.
The journey *takes* about three hours.

Sometimes both are possible with different meanings:

I *work* in a hospital
I *'m working* in a hospital

I do not plan to move soon – it is my permanent job.
I expect to move soon – it is a temporary job.

Where *do* you *live?*
Where *are* you *living?*

About your *permanent* home.
To a visitor, about his or her *temporary* home.

Where *do* you *go* for your holidays?
Where *are* you *going* for your holdiays?

Usually; general
This year; specific

Sometimes the objective difference is very small:

I *'m not feeling* very well.

I *don't feel* very well.

## Continuous forms      (be) + ... ing

All main verbs can occur in the simple or the continuous forms.

All continuous forms are made with *(be)* + ... *ing*.

The continuous form *always* means that the speaker, at the moment of use, draws particular attention to the fact that the action concerns a *limited period*.

|  | **Simple** | **Continuous** |
|---|---|---|
| **Present** | Where do you live? | Where are you living? |
| **Past** | What did you do? | What were you doing? |
| **Present passive** | It is printed in Birmingham. | It is being printed in Birmingham. |
| **Present perfect** | I've waited for three months. | I've been waiting for three months. |
| **'ll future** | I'll see him tomorrow. | I'll be seeing him tomorrow. |
| **going to** | I'm going to look at it tomorrow. | I'm going to be looking at it tomorrow. |

It is not a matter of *objective* fact. The continuous form shows the speaker's *subjective* interpretation of the facts.

## Present perfect and past simple

There are two different ways in English to talk about an event in the past:

> **The past simple suggests "then" or "at that time".**
> **The present perfect suggests "up to now" or "before now".**

| | |
|---|---|
| I first **met** John three years ago. | The speaker looks *at* the past event from the past, in a "flash back". |
| **I've known** John for three years. | The speaker looks *back* at the past event *from the present,* the moment of speaking. |

The facts described are the same. The speaker can use either verb form. The choice depends on the speaker's *subjective* view of the event.

The present perfect means that the past event is connected to the moment of speaking *in the speaker's mind.*

| | |
|---|---|
| I *haven't seen* David this morning. | (but it is still morning, so I might see him) |
| I *didn't see* David this morning. | (the morning is over, remote) |
| I *haven't seen* David yet. | (yet = up to now, so *I didn't see David yet* is impossible) |

Sometimes the difference is small:

| | |
|---|---|
| Yes, I *lived* there when I was a child. | (It is now remote from me) |
| Yes, I *'ve lived* there actually. | (You remind me NOW of something in the past) |

The perfect is *not* about the action being complete or not.
It is not always about the recent past.
The only general rule is the one given above.

**110**

# Index